# Hats Off

*poems by*

# Peter Waldor

*Finishing Line Press*
Georgetown, Kentucky

# Hats Off

Copyright © 2022 by Peter Waldor
ISBN 979-8-88838-048-2  First Edition
All rights reserved under International and Pan-American Copyright Conventions. No part of this book may be reproduced in any manner whatsoever without written permission from the publisher, except in the case of brief quotations embodied in critical articles and reviews.

Books by Peter Waldor

*Door to a Noisy Room*
*The Wilderness Poetry of Wu Xing*
*Who Touches Everything*
*The Unattended Harp*
*State of the Union*
*Gate Posts With No Gate*
*Nice Dumpling*
*Owl Gulch Elegies*
*Unmade Friend*
*Something About the Way*
*The Way 2*
*Midwife vs Obstetrician*

Publisher: Leah Huete de Maines
Editor: Christen Kincaid
Cover Art: Peter Waldor
Author Photo: Eric Trommer
Cover Design: Elizabeth Maines McCleavy

Order online: www.finishinglinepress.com
also available on amazon.com

Author inquiries and mail orders:
Finishing Line Press
P. O. Box 1626
Georgetown, Kentucky 40324
U. S. A.

# Table of Contents

Two Scouts ... 1
"Yo" ... 2
Oh Impure Contradiction! ... 3
Old Trail ... 4
Currants ... 5
Hats Off ... 6
Rites of Autumn ... 7
Bells ... 8
The Last Trail Crew ... 9
Peach ... 10
Every 250 Years ... 11
The Old Days ... 12
Tangled Itineraries ... 13
Common Thief ... 14
Long Time Partners ... 15
Spring In Fall ... 16
Mountains With Eyes Closed ... 17
Throat ... 18
Moss Campion ... 19
Discovery and Serenity ... 20
A Character About You ... 21
Provisional Note ... 22
Roll Away ... 23
Faded ... 24
Partners' Conundrum ... 25
Endless Wondering ... 26
In Passing ... 27
Not a Birder ... 28

Aging .................................................................................... 29

Pockets ................................................................................ 30

Under Over Around .......................................................... 31

Miners' Forgotten Candle ................................................. 32

Distant ................................................................................ 33

Sagging Tent ...................................................................... 34

Collector ............................................................................ 35

Tangled Light .................................................................... 36

Strange Cairns ................................................................... 37

Crystal ................................................................................ 38

Past Dusk ........................................................................... 39

Monkshood ....................................................................... 40

Near Death Experience ..................................................... 41

Rock the Father ................................................................. 42

Stone Trouble .................................................................... 43

Dig ...................................................................................... 44

Purple Fire Weed ............................................................... 45

Water Bottles ..................................................................... 46

Vision ................................................................................. 47

Wing ................................................................................... 48

Giant Pine .......................................................................... 49

Sharpening ........................................................................ 50

Bracted Lousewort ............................................................ 51

Blood .................................................................................. 52

Passing Hail storm ............................................................ 53

Hardening Mud ................................................................ 54

It Doesn't Occur To Me .................................................... 55

The Transition Time ......................................................... 56

Duty .................................................................................... 57

Bathing ............................................................................... 58

The Deplorables ................................................................ 59

*Walking with Marti Martin-Kuntz, David Kuntz and Lisa Allee*

## Two Scouts

We lose the old trail.
One woman scouts high.
One woman scouts low.
After they both vanish
we hear each of them
give a whoop, a signal
each found the trail.
We don't know which
to follow so we sit
on some rocks and chat.

## "Yo"

Long time partners,
one ahead of the other
on a high traverse.
The one behind yells
"Yo!" a signal to stop
and confer but the one
ahead, back to us,
merely raises a battered
walking stick,
shakes it like a rattle
and keeps walking.

## Oh Impure Contradiction!

In the crowd of deadfall
we scratch our chins
as we decide if a downed tree
was felled by people or nature.
The smooth end is ambiguous.
We try to get as far
from people as we can
but we hope that the cut
was made by a saw.

## Old Trail

By wind or time
all the blazed trees
were knocked down
so no one will
notice the gouges
that the trail crew
cut with a bunch of
easy hatchet strokes
except one who sees
one of the scars
on a fallen tree
She runs her palm
across the mark
as if it were letters
on an old grave

# Currants

My keen-eyed friends
notice some ripe currants
and stop to partake.
I feel like a city fool
for passing right by.
I had no idea currants
were everywhere
in the green understory,
but when I finally stop
to eat I worry about
the hungry bears
in this dry autumn.

## Hats Off

We all take our hats off when we get hot.
Some push our wet hair back,
others rub the magic balls of our scalps.
Little difference between us.

## Rites of Autumn

My love takes my last
piece of paper to fold
into a pouch as she collects
larkspur seeds, pinching
the black seeds out
of the rotted wafers
of flowers.  She scatters
a few seeds near the
skeletal stalks still standing
at attention as a trade
for taking some of the seeds
out of the forest,
but she is not too concerned
about her thievery.

## Bells

Walking across talus
the shifting rocks chime
under foot.
We never needed
forged bells.
These rocks ring clearer.
They have flaked
and fallen from the peaks.
I wonder how the
patchwork of lichens
effect the music,
as we strike
with our boots.
Once, at a museum,
behind a velvet rope,
I saw an ancient bell,
its faded copper
the same color
as the lichens.
We never needed
that bell,
let alone to shelter
it from time,
nor the prayers
it called
our ancestors to,
from their simple
dwelling places.

# The Last Trail Crew

It was an autumn dusk
on the last day of the
trail work season
when the woodsmen
sawed into four parts
a giant downed
spruce that had
fallen on the trail;
working together
they may have been
able to heave each
part off the trail,
but they didn't try
as it was getting dark
and they had a long
walk to camp.
They never returned
the next summer,
for the mine closed,
too expensive to extract
the remaining gold.
The bark is gone
from the giant rounds--
now bleached gray.
The old trail not even
a shadow of itself.
Today an ungulate
passes too close
and rubs its furry
flank against one
of the gray logs
and dreams
of the fallen
obelisks of Egypt.

## Peach

Stopping on some rocks
I watch my love eat
a peach and not offer
me a bite.  I am aghast.
She is the generous one
and I am the miser,
these thoughts just
one example of my
diabolical miserliness.

# Every 250 Years

Every other year
there is a storm
that wipes out
whole towns
along the coast,
washes the match
stick houses
into the sea;
and they say
it was a once
in a hundred year
event. I am afraid,
for my children,
that hundred year
events will happen
every year, or worse,
afraid in this giant stand
of ancient pines
blown down
a few days ago.

## The Old Days

Back in the day
the mine companies
clear cut the forests
going up to the peaks,
using the wood
for their occupations,
trestles and tracks,
dormitories, mills,
even a bowling alley
at 13,000 feet,
so it was just stumps
and wild flowers
along the high paths.
Now there is so much
deadfall in the thick
forests, it's nearly
impossible to pass
through to tree line
and peaks above.

## Tangled Itineraries

When the story teller
falls asleep mid-story,
the words tangle like twine.
We let him go
and watch the sky
quietly until we
too doze off.  Each on
a chosen stone.
Each sure not to press
against any moss,
too delicate
for biped heads.

# Common Thief

I thought the details
would absolve me
but now I realize
they'd only dig
my own grave
so suffice it to say
I stole the rare
lavender rose
chocolate I surprised
you with on the trail.
Guilt in an
innocent moment.
It's late autumn,
the king's crown
blossoms have
gone to seed
and vanished
but the leaves left
on the wobbly stems
are brighter red than the
blossoms ever were.
I am so sorry,
after all the living
you have done
you ended up with
a common thief.

# Long Time Partners

Long time partners
deep in the wilderness
and high above tree line.
They argue about
which way to go.
A serious argument
but it doesn't mean
a thing.  When one
complains about
the other interrupting
I intervene and tell them
the interruption is just
an opportunity for the
one interrupted to
bring up the old subject
one more time,
with fresh perspective.
Of course they don't
hear a word I say,
too busy arguing,
but they will be ok.
They both offer
to share their waters
because I am out.
The woman wants to
reach the saddle
below the spires
but doesn't hesitate
to retreat because
the man is spent.

## Spring In Fall

Three days of late
autumn snow melt
and in the runoff
and warm days
following a few
orange paintbrushes
have blossomed,
a youthful shock
in the yellow, brown,
and gray remains
of summer.
Spring in fall.
A few hundred feet
higher the snows haven't
melted and they won't,
for many months.
Short seasons,
no matter what
we call them.

## Mountains With Eyes Closed

Is it trails everywhere
or trails nowhere?
Or are you so tired
you close your eyes
and hear the answer
is "both," and with
eyes closed the snowy
peaks all around
are not seen, just felt,
as they prefer.
Shy giants.

# Throat

High above tree line
you find the throat
of an old whiskey bottle,
shaped like a dumbbell,
wide where the lips go
and wide where the
bottle once curved out
into its reservoir.
All that's left of a miner's
wild night, up on a steep slope
where broken rocks
are winning against
the alpine grasses.
You place the throat
back in the grasses,
in the same groove
you lifted it out of,
knowing it's best
to leave the primary
sources of history
undisturbed.

# Moss Campion

Long time partners
talk interminably about
the trails but it doesn't
mean they don't quiet
down for a group of elk
traversing the talus
a hundred yards higher.
The partners try to be
invisible but they
know they 're not.
In silence they notice
the moss campion,
smile and don't
say a word,
restraining themselves.
They see the flower's name
in each other's eyes.

## Discovery and Serenity

We find a battered canoe
on the Hope Lake shore.
One side of the hull
has the name "Discovery."
The other the name "Serenity."
The bow is cracked but not fatally,
and below "Discovery"
are instructions to strangers
to carry the canoe
fifty feet from the water
and leave it hull side up.
A boat with two names
too high up for anyone
to drag here.

# A Character About You

Because you were the fastest
female skier in the world,
and many other feats,
the local children's theatre
made a character about you
for a summer production.
You miscalculated
on opening night,
getting lost on the high
ridge line and drainages
dropping into Ophir,
making it back well past dark,
with no head lamp,
well after the play ended,
the empty front seat
they held for you, a missing
tooth in a grin.
Many years later, the record
changing hands and changing
hands, you don't even know
the name of the woman
who holds it now,
we descend the same
drainage and you recall
the missed play.
The child actors
are middle aged now,
sending their own children
to theatre camps,
not and never holding grudges.
Don't worry.

## Provisional Note

Making the topo map
for the Ophir quadrant
the surveyor penciled in
*interesting road* by
the broken line marking
the old road traversing
to the Suffolk Mine,
thinking he'd circle back
to give the road a name,
perhaps ask one
of the miners at the
Silver Jack Saloon
if they knew of it.
Somehow the map
made it to the printer with
that provisional note,
and so it became
indelible and now
seventy years later,
we unfold the map,
the fold lines
like quilting over
the well-used topo.
We see the name
*Interesting Road,*
and the road is,
indeed, interesting,
threading the gulleys
high above tree line,
on its rising traverse.

## Roll Away

Ahead of me
you roll away
a dead tree
I surmise
to clear my path
then I see three
saplings were pinned
under the trunk
Oh well
Oh good

## Faded

You spit on an old marker
and wipe the saliva across
the surface with your palm
bringing the faded letters
and numbers into relief,
all meaningless to us.

# Partners' Conundrum

Does one partner
follow the other
through the untouched
forest and have two
people beat down
the same places,
or do they fan out
so each makes
a lesser mark than
the two together?

## Endless Wondering

Wondering why
one tree fell
and not another
Endless wondering

## In Passing

Last year's buds
still tight on
a downed tree,
dozens,
gray capsules,
close to the
ground,
within reach.
You hold one
in your palm
a moment,
in mourning,
in passing.

## Not a Birder

Though you know some
bird names you don't
have expensive
binoculars or a glossy
pocket North American
Field Guide and no
friends like that either
You simply stop
to look at the birds
for a long time
no matter how far
ahead we wander

# Aging

Aging I notice
more clearly
the first sprigs of spring,
even the smallest
most humble blades,
and no worries
with the passing
thought that this
will happen
without me soon.

## Pockets

A woman doesn't
say to herself
*time to take
my hands out of
my pockets now,*
they just pop out
when the slope
gets loose and steep;
they find those
invisible bars
to grip for dear life.

# Under Over Around

Sapling growing
under over around
a giant fallen tree
If all goes well
it'll grow up
and no one
will know why
it took so many
strange turns
as the fallen
elder will vanish
as they all do

## Miners' Forgotten Memories

Abandoned wheelbarrows
dotting the high wilderness,
all crushed and splayed.
Dreams of gold in their
rusting cavities or at least
in miners' forgotten memories.

# Distant

In the wilderness people talk
of their distant families.
Distant in space, time, or love.
You tell us your father's plane
was shot down over North Korea
when your mother
was pregnant with you.
The men always gained weight
on his side of the family
but he was still the dashing
young aviator. Rather than
throw away his spare survival bag
you cut and stitched it
into a vest, seventy years later.
No time at all.

## Sagging Tent

One man tent sagging
in the wild, muddy
corn cob pipe,
cans, fry pan,
scattered about.
We shake the faded
orange nylon;
maybe there's a body
inside, it's hard to tell
the weight.
We don't unzip it.
We walk away.

# Collector

All those years going
into the wilderness
you found precious
artifacts from the
old mining days,
bowls and bottles,
purple electrical
insulators, fry pans
and canteens.
You left them
undisturbed,
where they were
abandoned,
for future explorers
or aliens to
marvel at.
Years later you
returned to some
of these remote sites
and saw the
treasures were gone.
You would have been
the better collector.

## Tangled Light

Light tangled in
fountains of grass,
like golden hair
tangled in golden hair.

How many tens
of thousands of years
ago did we start
experimenting
with hair?

Is this today
or my earliest
childhood memory?

Friends ahead.
Even though I can't
think of a thing
to say I love
to hear them talk.
Eventually they'll wait,
though I hope it's
not for a while.

## Strange Cairns

Cairns every
now and then
but not a trail.
No direction.
Burial mounds?
Was there a battle?
They are so covered
with lichens
they could be
giant buds waiting
for the right
light and heat
to blossom.

## Crystal

You found a curved
quartz crystal half
out of the earth.
Heart shaped
or a jaw,
depending on
who looks.
Without hesitation
you point me
towards it
and help me lash
it to my pack.
Months later,
when you
asked about that
rock I sensed
envy had eaten
away at your great
generosity so I
left it on your stoop
last night. It was
good to be with it
a few months
of its huge life.
Enjoy. It shines
with no plug.

## Past Dusk

In the little turnout
below Ophir Crag
we find an old truck
at the trail head.
The climbers
should have
long decamped
from the cliffs.
We didn't think
much about it
but later
we worried and
walked back to get
the license number
for the rangers.
The truck was gone.

# Monkshood

I'm lucky enough to point out
the first monkshood of summer.
I'd like to break off a few blossoms
and eat them and die a slow
and painful death but I don't want
to hurt the plants.

# Near Death Experience

The giant rock slide
stopped as mysteriously
as it started and we
merely ended up
fifty feet down the slope,
just cuts and bruises,
nothing twisted,
nothing broken.

It is a crime to come
close to death,
and to, at least temporarily,
enjoy life more afterwards;
for the right way to
enjoy life is without
any death brushes.

# Rock the Father

High up you dance
from rock to rock,
skipping over
the flowers
so your boots
won't crush them.
Not realizing
the humiliation
the rock feels,
like the child
having his head
forced close to
the spilled milk
by his father.
Worse. Because
the rock is
supposed to be
the father.
Rock the father.

## Stone Trouble

You picked up a stone
and couldn't find a spot
to put it back down,
even the old spot
didn't seem right.
So it goes in a pocket.

## Dig

You stare at a wave
of downed and bent trees,
to deduce the origin
and severity of a past avalanche.
I'd like to make a dig
and say you're too preoccupied
to notice the splendor
but I'd be mistaken,
and the destruction itself
after all is part
of the splendor.

## Purple Fireweed

shimmers
in the detritus
of a months
old avalanche.
First off it's not
purple but pink,
the greatest of colors;
second of all
it's not a weed.
What could be
more choice among
the florals?
As the pinks rise
in the deadfall
we can see time
pass and we can
see time doesn't
exist at all.

## Water Bottles

We met a man
in the wilderness.
I call him lonely,
but I don't know.
He had no water.
I debated whether
to give him one
of my two bottles
but decided
against it since
he didn't ask.
When I opened
my pack later I saw
my second bottle
was gone.

# Vision

Is that a crumpled tissue
or a lily blossom fallen
on the trail? If I retreat
it will just be a white
smudge. If I go closer
I will see the answer.
I hold still as I can so I
can give you exactly
what I am not sure I see.

# Wing

Longtime partners
tramp through some snow.
Sometimes one says
what the other is thinking.
Sometimes one catches
the other by surprise.
They stop for short rests,
all they allow themselves.
Though they have had
their share of misfortune
they are both close
to weeping for
a butterfly wing
lodged in the snow,
the wing's dark colors
attract the light
so it sinks into
an ever deepening
white flake bowl.

# Giant Pine

So big the tree
itself is a green sky
and the dots of sky
poking through
the needles
are the stars.

## Sharpening

Fresh claw marks
all over the aspen
tree neighborhood.
Bear claws.
The sleep is done
and it's time for
sharpening. It's nice
to see all the new
gashes, nice not
to see the bear.

# Bracted Lousewort

I say it's a bracted lousewort,
so quick to go to seed
many plant lovers
just call it a DYC
(damn yellow composite)
or you says it's
an elephant's head
(wrong shape and color),
another says
miner's candle
(everything wrong.)
But those sagging
yellow fins, so pale
one argues they
are white, are flags
of no country.
They deserve a name.
They are a prayer
that there will be
a time with no flags
and no countries,
just names of flowers,
and that time is not
the end of days
but the beginning.

## Blood

Amazing how with all the creatures
in the wilderness, predators and prey
and otherwise, how little, if any,
blood we've seen in all our walking.

## Passing Hail Storm

One of us shelters
under a large tree during
a hail storm, another
stands in a clearing
to be pelted,
holding an arm
over her eyes.
Or are we
the same people
on different days.
.

## Hardening Mud

Elk hoof print gouged
inches into the hardening mud.
Doubtful conditions will lend
it a few million more
years of form, but we'll
at least get a few days,
which is almost as long
for the thoughtful elk.

# It Doesn't Occur To Me

A small bird, a sparrow?
hops in front of me,
hovering, small flights,
as if trying to escape
but I am on the same path
so I keep right behind it.
Finally I say, in English,
*little bird go to one*
*side or another and*
*you'll be free of me.*
It doesn't occur to me
to go to one side
or another, myself.

## The Transition Time

We each pick and give
the other what we pick,
wild strawberries,
into the other's
palm or mouth,
both of us unsure
of the transition time,
when we keep our
pickings for ourselves.

# Duty

Our duty—
to walk
the old trails
no longer
on maps,
to keep
them alive,
to show
no one.

# Bathing

Is it unfair that I bathed
after our day in the wilderness
and you didn't, that I love
to be "clean" for you and
for you to be "dirty?"
That this is how I dream
of us together and this
is how we are after
a day finding hidden
waterfalls with dear friends;
one water ladder above
the other all the way
up the mountain
to the snow field
not quite glacier anymore.

## The Deplorables

Getting on the highway
after a long hike up
the Old Hope Lake Trail,
a chain of Harleys,
passing cars, cross
onto my side and I
swerve onto the shoulder
to miss them.
I can't help but think,
though there is little
difference between
humans, these are the
deplorables that
Hillary Clinton, who won
the 2016 election
by 3,000,000 votes,
so bravely called out.
I scream out the window
and try to give the
bikers the finger
but it's been so long
I forgot, briefly, which
finger it was and they
were gone before
I remembered.

**P**eter Waldor is the author of twelve books of poetry, including *Who Touches Everything*, which won the National Jewish Book Award. He was the Poet Laureate of San Miguel County, Colorado for 2014-2015. His poetry has appeared widely in magazines, including the *American Poetry Review, Ploughshares, The Colorado Review, Fungi Magazine* and *Mothering Magazine.* He lives in Ophir, Colorado.

www.ingramcontent.com/pod-product-compliance
Lightning Source LLC
Chambersburg PA
CBHW031127160426
43192CB00008B/1135